Poems

of

Angst and Awe

In Four Acts

Published 2017
Printed in The United States of America

For permission requests or information, please address the author at GITABAACK.COM

Cover Photograph - Personal Collection Gita Baack.

Arian Baack, Gita, author
    Poems of angst and awe / Dr. Gita Arian Baack.

Issued in print and electronic formats.

ISBN 978-1-77302-739-5 (softcover).--ISBN 978-1-77302-741-8 (PDF)

    I. Title.

PS8601.R485P64 2017   C811'.6   C2017-902968-1
                                      C2017-902969-X

www.tellwell.ca

Dedicated to my parents Sam and Lea Arian
They couldn't have loved me less.

"A poet is a naked person
– some people say I'm a poet."

~ Bob Dylan

An Invitation to "Poems of Angst and Awe"

I invite you to step away from the world outside, and sit with this book of poems for a while. You may sit and reflect on a particular poem or roam around and dip into different poems. Regardless of your reactions to the poems, notice what comes up for you in your world. I hope as a result, you are touched, inspired or helped in some way.

About my process

I write poems when I have strong feelings or am puzzling over a concept. You will find an undercurrent of various forms of humour in many of these poems, even those that are written from a painful place. After all, laughter is often really so close to tears, soothing the scars of life.

Once I have written in a spontaneous way, I go back repeatedly—paring down what I have written, deleting any words that seem unnecessary or that seem not sincere enough. Eventually, I am at a place closer to the core of what is going on. Somehow, when I get to that core, I feel released, able to stand more steadily and see more clearly.

Why 'angst' and 'awe' in four acts?

I barely thought of the title; it came to me suddenly. Afterwards, I realized that the two constructions, angst and awe, are really a good fit with my view of the world as one full of contradictions, without any black and white answers. Angst contains a combination of the unbearable anguish of life constantly striving to overcome this seemingly impossible situation. I use awe in the sense of amazement, not fear or reverence. The world's wonders surprise me constantly -- the beauty of nature, children, sexuality, laughter, the beauty of faces in all their differences. I am also in awe when I experience unexpected epiphanies, realizations that can leave me laughing or awestruck, happy in the moment of discovery.

What you will find in the four acts?

The book is organizing into four acts as a metaphor for the stage upon which we play out our life.

The poems in Act 1, "Burdens and Lightness of Youth", are about the angst of youth, a time when we create our identity, leave home, build relationships, experience loss and fulfillment, experiment with life, and discover both the anguish and wonders of life. I have been writing poetry since I was about 12-years old so these poems cover many topics from the burdens of family difficulties, school, feelings of isolation, as well as those joyful times when the load of our burdens are lightened by all kinds of craziness.

The poems in Act 2, "Life in General", are a snapshot of my experiments with relationships, ideas, and strivings to become someone special. It is a small buffet with a mixture of tastes, sweet, bitter and the in-between.

In the poems of Act 3, "Unrequited Love", I openly share my poems written over a lifetime of the angst and awe of my relationships with men. I love the quote by Gabriel Garcia Marquez:
"I became aware that the invincible power
that has moved the world is unrequited, not happy, love."
Indeed, unrequited love is a common experience, evident in song, theatre, film, visual art, dance and writings throughout time.

The poems of Act 4, "Maybe", are more of awe and less of angst as I explore what is possible in the world of relationships with oneself, other people, and the world—maybe.

Contents

Act 2 Life in General

Act 3   Unrequited Love

Act 4   Maybe

Act 1

Burdens
and Lightness
of Youth

Shhh, listen ...

A little, little, person
Sat in his little, little, chair
Singing the song of the seas

Whistling through the winds
Above the din of the world
The little, little, person
Can be heard
If you take a little time
To listen to his little tune.

Daddy's Home

It's six o'clock
Time for Daddy to come home
There's a fumbling at the lock
That's him, that's him.
A cold glow surrounds
The man who has brought
Karnartzel* and cakes and chewing gum.

He blushingly watches our joyful acceptance
Of his offerings of love
Before even taking his coat off.

* A kind of beef jerky

Careful Place

When I was ten
I found a baby bird
I put it in a careful place
The next day I heard
He had been eaten
By a friendly neighbourhood cat
Only I cared enough to cry.

        I wanted to be a bird
        But a cat ate me.

once I saw a pwetty bug

Once I saw a pwetty bug
    As pwetty as can be

    I gave him a wittle kiss
        But he got dead as dead can be.

The Spider and the Apple Cider

Once upon a kitchen chair
I sat with wondrous bones and hair
For I espied a spider
Crawling into my apple cider.

Then the spider turned to mesh
As I killed him with one smash
But he never knew what hit him
Not before, not during
Nor after, I did him in.

And so my story ends
I'm sorry
I didn't mean to be so glum
But would you like some of my apple cider?
And glutton that I am

I'm thirsty evermore!

Invisible

I am an invisible child
Hiding
Behind my doubts

Unseen, unacknowledged, unknown
Not real.

I can't see much
There seems to be a river
Where I sense I can be made real
It's around the corner
Around the wall
But then disappears
And becomes invisible
Just like me.

Talking, Not-Talking

I got a good one
Around my tongue
It's hiding 'neath
The tonsil tree.

I think I'll just keep it there
In case no one
Listens to me.

Knowing, Not-Knowing

I've gone to the moon
But forgot what I saw
But I know there is something
More

I've yet to find
What I'm looking for
But I know there is more
Because I have gone to the moon.

outbursts

I can
Because I want to
So I will
If I don't
It's because I don't want to
So I won't.

Laughter, laughter all around
But not a smile to spare.

Thank you for the nylon fluorescent shirt
It's two sizes too big
And has a colour I can puke on.

You are a Shit
So am I.

If
I die
It won't be
my fault.

Void

Snakes wriggling down slopes
green brown dun dirt
downintothenarrowing
downintothenarrowing
black individual pits
they bury themselves
into the black
into the void
into

Stoned No. 1

Must my mind
Remain in state
Number four
No! My mind can soar
Where it will
Where all is still
With sound and thought.

Stoned No. 2

My face immersed in a cup
All is circumscribed
So, drink up!

The cup on my head
No longer can I see
My face looking back at me

And now my mind can soar
For I can see much more.

Stoned No. 3

Alone with the radio
In this strange dark room
I must eat and smoke and write

Yes, I must write
Organs aren't enough
Where is my mind
Mind come back!

Oh, you're back
Hi mind
Hi girl
See you later.

Stoned No. 4

Boy me stoned ha, ha
Room playing tricks
Table gets in way of
Cigarette
        and falls to my bed
Aaaaaaaagh!!!!!

Stoned No. 5

Me
look at clock, it says 3:00
But Me
knows it's 10:00
ha, ha
But my Buddha
laughs at me

Radio says don't get excited
And picture on wall shows
All hands up in air shrieking
Whoops — now room playing
Hide-and-seek
It see it not.

Stoned No. 6

Blank on this side
Gee
Under tweezers, razor blade, pen
Chocolate paper

And under that is deep

And above that is high
Telephone rings.

I jump

       p

   u

 &&

   d

     o

       w

         n

Not for me
High no longer so important.
Deep no longer so important.

Stoned No. 7

You curse
    You helpmate

You pollute my nerves
    shatter my calmness

    Calm my nerves
        restore my existence

Communications are made easier with your help.

    "Would you like a cig?"
    "Sure thanks"

Such a nice gesture of friendship!

"Come on, baby let's fuck."
    "Wait, I have to have a cigarette first."

Hey where did you go, cigarettes?
Got to get some more.
Get the pennies out of the piggybank.
Piggy on my back
Such a stinky piggy you are.

Stoned No. 8

Light creeping over
The ridge of my window
Touches my sweater
On the chair, the wall
The back of my head
Is inside my head
And puts me to sleep
As I am wide awake.

My friend karol

giggle bubble gurgle jurgle
trouble hubble toil swubble
go   come
run   walk
fun
only with an equal one.

Jacqueline (Jackie) and John F. Kennedy

November 22, 1963

John Kennedy was shot!
Everyone heard the shot!

I was in my late teens celebrating
It was my birthday the next day
I was dancing with my handsome
And so brilliant boyfriend
I was so proud, so happy.

On the outside at least
Inside I was so afraid
How would I survive if he abandoned me?

Then the loud speakers told
the dancing university students
"John Kennedy was shot!"

It was Jackie that taught me how I would survive
It was Jackie that changed me forever.

"Imagine that!' I said to myself
A woman
Doesn't have to fall apart
And turn into nothing
Even as she is covered in His blood
Even after burying her babies
Even after losing Camelot.
She can stand fully present
For herself, for her children
Even for her country.

Martin Luther King

April 5, 1968

I bled last night
Martin Luther King has died here after I bled last night.
Prematurely for me
Prematurely for his people
Prematurely for the world.

Robert F. Kennedy

June 5, 1968

History bleeds again
and again, and again and again and again and again
and again and again and again and again and again
and again and again and again and again and again
and again and again and again and again and again
and again and again and again and again and again
and again and again and again and again and again
and again and again and again and again and again
and again and again and again and again and again
and again and again and again and again and again
and again and again and again and again and again
and again and again and again and again and again
and again and again and again and again and again
and again and again and again and again and again
and again and again and again and again and again
and again and again and again and again and again
and again and again and again and again and again
and again and again and again and again and again
and again and again and again and again and again
and again and again and again and again and again
and again and again and again and again and again
and again and again and again and again and again
and again and again and again and again and again
and again and again and again and again and again
and again and again and again and again and again
and again and again and again
and again and again
and again

Song of Gita

I am a bird woman
Circling the world
Seeking solace
From the sorrowful notes
That beat without measure
Reverberating from one heart to the next.

I sing to myself as I fly
I sing to myself as I cry
My own song of Gita

Known only by me
Understood alone by me.

At night, I tuck myself under my wing
And find comfort there
A pause from the endless
Meaningless refrains.

My Mother has Two Sisters

My mother has two sisters
Called Doubt and Disappointment

Their dark shadows hover around me
At my every turn
Always nearby
Nattering in my mind.

"Be careful
Better watch out
You'll be disappointed
You'll cry

You don't know enough
You're not strong enough
You're not pretty enough
You're not smart enough

You'll cry, you'll cry."

Posture

I keep my head
Sticking out from my neck
Like someone expecting
To have it chopped off

I keep my head
Sticking out from my neck
Like someone on the alert
To oncoming danger

I keep my head bowed
Like a humble monk
Not knowing what face
To project to the world

I would like to take my head
In my hands
Like Ichabod Crane
And put it back
Straight

So no one would know
What really goes on
In my misaligned
Self

So no one would know
I was so scared and unsure.

A Mute Appeal

Help the giver of my life
Help the taker of the death
And Life I deal to her

Stop up her heart at the penalty
Of stagnation
Stop it up anyway.

Me and You

When I was me
I could laugh at you
even though I sweat

Now I'm you
And you laugh at me
While I sweat more.

To my brother, Morris

Dignified and Pathetic
You stand my brother
But when All are you
And you are All
Thou shalt reap
What thou hast sown
And your sweat will
Become the dew on the
Brow of wee flowers.

Dating No. 1

bite, scratch, dig, claw, pull
try to get to his soul
emotion surges, a smell foul
erupts
no path have you dug
his soul remains intact.

try another man
bite, scratch, dig, claw, pull
he, too, is hard to fool
if he wants to remain whole,
he can.

we must not delay
timeisgettingon
you must elaborate your female play
bite harder scratch sharper dig deeper pull apart
you are only playing with a human heart.

Dating No. 2

Can't ever pet you like a dog or cat.
Can't you drop dead?
Go to hell where you belong.
You'll feel much better there then in my
lungs, heart, vagina.

You think you're clever don't you
Disguising yourself in God's colour
But you can't hide the black smoke, the flares
that burn within you

I see through you.
I'll drown you yet.
Just you wait and see.

Where the hell are those dammed cigarettes?

Dating No. 3

Hi Paul,
Would you like to play ball?
If you do,
I'll be your best friend.

But if you don't,
Or if you lose it,
Or if you'll play with someone else,
I'll hate you forever.

Dating No. 4

You could drown
Goliath melancholy
If you would

I could turn your indolence
Into love's magnificence
Of wholeness and oneness
If you would
Desire Me.

Dating No. 5

Don't burden me with your cares
I bear them already.

Don't burden me with your woes
I've wept over them already.

Don't burden me with your fears
I've quaked over them already.

Don't burden me with your needs
I've wanted them already.

How old Before You Know

How old before you know
    how to feel love's sea
    without a youth's ideology
    or truths proclaimed with false passions
    of adults in their moral fashions

How old before it is too late
    To fill
    The empty spaces
    With a lover's embraces
    And kisses of beloved faces
    And words of kindness easing
    Harsh everyday places

How old before you know
    Who took your innocence away
    And screwed you royally
    On top of the balcony
    And as you fell
    Below
    And found it on the way
    Because you like to play
    I've got one more line to say.

Punished and Banished

We are punished
For our failings, frailties and fears
If not by our own self-loathing selves
We find someone who will
Finish us off
Far fucking out
Damn self
Out
Damn
Selffffffffffffffffffffffffffffffffffffffffff

O U T!

Classroom

Just look at these sensual beings
Writing an exam they'll soon forget
Blowing and panting
And running their hands
Through
The fog of the mind
When only the body is interesting
Encompassing
Wanting

Seventeen and squirming
Pimpled and protruding
Soon to be cleansed
Soon to be sullied
Soon to be misshapen
No longer wanting anything

But oh, how gorgeous they are
Today
Wanting
In their too tight pants
And their too tight shirts
Their undisciplined hair
Their expectant faces.
Soon to be disappointed.

Apologies to the instructors, to my class and to Leonard Cohen

The walls of this classroom are paper thin
I've been disoriented since I walked in
One whole morning late
It seemed to seal my fate
My apologies to Marilyn, Don and this great class
No books, no instruments
I'm a real pain in the ass

But today is another day,
Et je pense
It can only get better with a new start
In La Belle Province.*

*The Province of Quebec is known as "La Belle Provence"

Touch Creates

his hand touches
tingling, swaying, dizzying, whirling, swooping,
reds, yellows moving, swirling, swinging

t
 h
  o
   u
    g
    h
     t

     s
      h
       a
       t
       t
        e
        r
        s

my body is numb
colour of blue.

on Dave's Beautiful Moustache

The beardless businessmen
Have too long betrayed our bards
And yielded to the feminine foe
And her selfish, crooked cards.
Alone Dave plays the deathly game
To win back honour to man's heavenly frame.

Dave slaps and packs these sweet men of woes
To stop the female's uncompromising blows.
The sweet male babe no longer needs mourn
A future of continued scorn
He'll grow to be big of body and of distinctive sex
Virile and wise, without any castration complex.

True to his conscience, Dave will not heed
The modern barbarian's creed:
>   *Work, work, and give all to womankind*
>   *With that alone will come peace of mind.*
No, Dave exclaims, COME, COME you all
And follow my decree
A moustache above a tough lip and she'll
Fall to her knees.

She'll love you and beg and crawl,
For your pleasures
No man needs succumb
To another's authority.
COME, COME,
This is for our posterity
We'll fight the sweet men along with the women if need be
The world must be dominated by HE and not she.

The Death of Marcello

Marcello, my pretty
Blue, blue fish
Has died
After eight months
Of swimming
Around
And
Around
In his little, little bowl

He had no choice
In his little, little life
He lived according to my command
Until he died

It was his one independent act

He showed me
At last
Who was really in control

So sad
So sad

I feel so bad
So bad.

Conversations

Pretty is a pretty word, I just heard it.
Ruin isn't, I just heard it too.
Talking people around me.
Something
I can't forget
But I can't remember it either.
What does all this talking mean anyway?

If it says
Something
Say it louder please
So I can hear it too.
So that I will remember it.
This time.
Maybe next time?

Nobody believes anybody.
Nobody even believes themselves
Sometimes, anytime, all the time.

Play offs.
That's a funny word.
Who is playing and off of what?
Are all these words playing off each other?

Where do they go blowing to
These billions of words in the air
There really isn't enough room
For all these words.

Are they really something?
If they are really something,
Please let me hear it too.

Act 2

Life in General

Innocence

Innocence played
Alone

And when joined
By others

Play became
Work

And Innocence
Was lost to those arrivals

And Innocence became anxious
And Anxious began to fight

Fighting became hurtful
Hurtful began hurting

And forgot Innocence.

A Long Time to Now

Hi Love,
I've been waiting for you
A long time.

So glad you came
Would you come some more
Do you have a lifetime
Of coming
To me?

I'll be here waiting you know
If you like
I'll come
Too
To you.

So glad we didn't get lost
On all those different paths
Each of us
Could have taken
Shall we go
Together
Now?

The Tiger who was a Snake

Away on a jaunt
What do you spread?
Tastes of onion soup meant to haunt
And spaghetti sauce
And wine so sweet
And knowledge of what's good to eat.
And knowledge of what's good to eat.

Away on the prowl
What do you devour?
Fowl who cannot fly
From your foul wisdom's heat
Of knowledge of what's good to eat.
Of knowledge of what's good to eat.

Untitled No. 1

I am spinnier than thou
And whirly images
Circulate up the spiral
Guts of my brain
And as they go round
And round until I think
I shall go mad
Suddenly
They sink into the whirlpool
Of my heart
And there begin to
Gnaw.

So this is Life

The sun is blindingly bright
The moon is jaundiced yellow
And the trees don't sway
They're trying to grab something
But cannot reach it
They can't even get away.

The neurotic chattering of birds
As they catch their worms
Are reminiscent of our neurotic chattering
before the worms catch us.

Your arms don't encircle
They engulf
As does the one and many
Deaths
Of our one Life.

wrapped up

I love you
Is a meaningless phrase
Let's tell it like it is

We are wrapped up in
Our neuroses

We cling to each other
but get no support
Because we can't hold ourselves up

We hide from ourselves
We have no guarantees
To give each other
And we're afraid to ask.

I'm Mad at You

Michael is a pompous
    overbearing
    egotistical
    super moody
    spoiled child

who won't lift a finger for anybody unless they are,
in his view, his superior or equal.

If you think I'm wrong it's because you're a pompous
                overbearing
                egotistical
                super moody
                spoiled child

who won't lift a finger for anybody unless they are
in your view, your superior or equal

Signed
                a maudlin
                weak
                goody goody martyr
                monotonous
                spoiled child

who hates you to-day but is cooking for you with care anyway
because she's
                a maudlin
                weak
                goody goody martyr
                spoiled and soiled
                woman.

I'm Mad at You Again

You are non-supportive
Critical
And consequently
Insulting

You can be supportive
Approving
And consequently
Loving

And if you won't allow
Us to go on forwards
We will quickly revert
To where we were
And I'll be on guard
And I'll be vulnerable
But I will not be destroyed and
I will not let you destroy me.

whoring

Our souls have been torn out
By loving people

We have become whores
Prostituting ourselves
To trivialities

We have allowed twisted
Minds to twist our hearts
Until the dissonant beats
Clang into our ears
And make us
Mad.

Ottawa Waspland

Awesomely mundane
Pathetically cowardly
Afraid
Doing its rounds
Around and around.

The Song of the Bureaucrat

I have no heart
I have no soul,
But it's okay,
I have control.

When I win the Lottery

When I win the lottery...
The LOT tery
The Lot of my life
Will hold no more

"Why did all this have to happen to me?"

"Why can't that happen to me"?

"Why can't I win the lottery"?

what happened to me?

I saw it coming.
I knew it was going to happen.
I have a husband
I have a child
I forgot to expect myself
What happened to me?

A Series of outbursts

I wanted to be a lady

But I went and had a baby.

I wanted to fly and soar

But I couldn't find the floor.

I wanted to be rich

but I didn't have the money.

So what?

So?

What?

Time No. 1

nervous shattering of flesh
thedeboningofthe newborn child
maybe one day maybe one hundred days
maybe 32,000 days
maybe one million days old

      a child as yet in foundling clothes
      undiscovered
      and wailing

once discovered no more to be found
such mingling
of times
makes for such a stinking broth.

Time No. 2

I'm afraid I will be trapped in Today
Tomorrow will remain
Jammed
In the machine of time
The grinding wheels will stop in the midst of rolling over me

Time — it's impossible to live without you
Your ever-changing medicine
Poured over the poison of sameness
Liquidates.
And so I bless and embrace the nothing
You so mercifully produce.

The mundane world of the little woman

toilets and toilet training
cooking and garbage
clean filth

   of house and mind

the pot of the husband, the pot of soup and the poteeee of

   the baby

making dreams of golden pots
of golden bellies

and lots and lots of don't know whats.

Poor baby

Poor baby
Too, too, bad
It hurts I know
And no reason
To show

Poor baby
Too bad
It hurts I know.

To my little son

Baby
            Baaaybeee
How are you sweetheart?

If you're not fine
            Just fine

ALL RIGHT
ALL IN ALL, ALL RIGHT

Then nothing is
And nothing will be.

Please BE
Please BE Well
Please BE Happy
Because if you're not
JUST RIGHT
Nothing IS.

My Daughter, Myself

Daughter	**Mother**
Don't give me advice She said	I cannot judge you Because you are me
Give me support She said	Everything you are doing I have done Forty years more
Understand my pain She said	Everything you are feeling I have felt Forty years more
Love me No matter what She said	You are me as I am you No matter what
Don't judge me For I am but A woman growing Up.	I too ask not to be judged For you see, I too am a woman Growing Into life's unexpected ups and downs.

Projecting

You get yourself into shit
I bail you out
You look at me and yell:

"Mom, can't you see,
There's shit all over you,
You're disgusting."

Untitled No. 2

Long shadow on my short tomb
Still
Beats the heart
Flies to the one-eyed moon
Why
The warriors weep below.

Act 3

Unrequited Love

Marlene and Me

"Falling in love again
What am I to do
never wanted to
I can't help it."

*Composed by Frederick Hollander and
Sammy Lerner, 1930, sung by Marlene Dietrich

Shopping

My Lover
and I
went shopping

He bought Many
things

I bought
no   thing

I gave Him
all my money.

The Sinking Sensation of Disappointment

The longest roller coaster drop
Cannot compare
With the stomach churning
Heart crunching
Eye stinging
Sinking sensation of
Disappointment.

Were my expectations too high?
Isn't it right?
Isn't it safe?
Isn't it fair?

If you answer
   "No — don't expect,
   It isn't right
   It isn't safe
   There is no fair."

My tears will wash away your bitter words
And my heart will shout:
      "No — I demand to expect
      It must be right; I'll make it safe
      There must be fair."

I'll chance that ride
That up-and-down-ride
With more downs than ups
More tears than smiles.
I won't let it, show I won't tell
I'll take a chance, and tell you Go to Hell.

Still Love Wanting

I want the After, while we are
Still
In the Before
As I will want the Before
When we will be in the After

With one kiss, time disappears
One more kiss, and I know another you
The innocent boy; the worried father
The sweet man; the bitter man

Each kiss brings one more of you to
Love
Each kiss finds another part of me
I thought was gone
I want them all.

I see your kind face
Head cocked to one side
Studying all that goes by
Wondering, "Do I dare to want?"
Then I hear a whispered, "I want…"

Forgiving one another for the aching pain
Sure to come with
Wanting.

Memorandum To Myself

I cannot allow myself to lose control
I should not let her touch my soul
The future must be clear to me
I cannot let myself be free

I fear the pain
My love, her love
Will bring, again and again

I cannot sing love songs
For a love that should not be
Should not, could not
Rule the day
Should not, could not
Is the only way
To expel the pain and passion
I cannot allow love to just happen.

The Time In-Between

Nothing seems real
During the Time
In-between
When your mouth is on mine
When your hands are on my body
Not even me
As if
I'm in between
The candle and the flame.

Our Magic

I love the way you look at me ...
    with your eyes
    with your mouth
    with your voice

That voice....
    The catch in your voice, that tells me of your desire,
    The sadness in your voice, that tells me of your need
    The hesitation in your voice
    that tells me
    of a wish not to bear
    such longing
    such need.

That raspiness in your voice ...
    that speaks to me of a man's passion
    so real
    so hard to ignore.

        How those looks, that voice
        Move me to my very being
        And make me yearn to fill
        The emptiness inside of you
        Inside of me
        With love's magic potion
        A blend of all that is you, and all that is I
        Uniquely ours.

Love's Creation

Love's creation is at once both
Naked and vulnerable
Open to the primal energy force
That brings us as close to beauty as we can get.

It is also clothed in a suit of armor
Protected from the world
Of danger and threats.

How difficult it is to differentiate
The creator from the created
Each one taking imperceptible turns
At making the perfect form

That comes alive
Under loving hands
That becomes free and strong
Fired by a giving heart.

Shades of Danger and Promise

My love brings me many shades of yellow
Dark, roadside yellow warning of danger ahead
Watch out!
Don't cross!
It's not safe!

But I'm already running across
Smiling bravely
Pretending not to be afraid
It's true — it isn't safe
But it's too late
I was once told if you're in the middle of the road
It's more dangerous to run back
Than it is to run forward

And so, I run ahead
Because I've known the
Golden warmth of his hands
His honeyed kisses
The intense glow between us when we make love

The yellow glint in his eyes betrays him
It calls out to me
Yes, come
There is some happiness here after all

And all fear disappears
A quiet amber light
Surrounds us
Protects us
And makes us safe
At least for now.

Should Has No Options

Should makes things hard on you and me
I know you're doing your best
And I don't ask for more

The way you love me now
Is all that I ask
It's a wonderful love
And I cherish it
I wouldn't do anything to disturb its' delicate balance

We are between two worlds
Our options are few
But we have at least one option
To go on, loving each other as we do
But if it gets too hard
I'll understand
And I won't think any less of you
I'll simply love you as always
And miss you.

The Eternal Husband

The anxiety that is himself
The eternal husband
Paralyzed by fear of the unknown
Has unknowingly created
A prison of the known
From which he cannot escape

A failed middle-aged attempt
At feeding the man,
The joys of a boy
Only finds him back
In the desert of his despair

He looks through his blackened window
Gnawing at his nails
But cannot see
Confused
Body aching
For a soothing touch
The eternal husband
Muffles his scream of discontent.

The Eternal Beloved

The anxiety that is herself
The eternal beloved
Paralyzed by fear of being alone
Has unknowingly created
The state of solitude
From which she longs to escape

A failed middle-aged attempt
At feeding the woman,
The joys of youth
Only finds her back
In the desert of her despair

She looks hopefully thru her lit win
Face drawn with worry and fatigue
But cannot see him
Confused
Body aching
For a soothing touch
The eternal beloved
Muffles her scream of longing.

Let's Make a Deal

Let's make a deal, Darling
You can go
When you know
What colour my eyes are.

I am a little bird on his shoulder

I am a little bird on his shoulder
Singing, whispering, teasing and laughing
In his ear

When he whistles his familiar love song
I fly to him
And tuck myself into the curve of his neck
As close to him as I can get
Skin to skin
Heart to heart
Lips to lips

I am his yellow bird offering happiness
Always sitting on his shoulder
Always with him
As he is with me.

New Love, Love Anew

Why do I love you?
Is it really love?
How long will it last?
Will you hate me when it's over?
Will you remember me?

You need to know the answers to those questions
So that you can trust yourself to let go
So that you can trust me not to abandon you,
As you once were so long ago

Passion turned to love, love to passion
I don't know how

I know I hunger to be fed
By the Us that we become together
And I wilt when we're apart

I know my love will keep
Long after the world intrudes
And I know a part of me will die

I don't know much else
I don't know if that's enough
For now, the answer is simply

Yes!

I Haven't Been Listening

I haven't been listening
To what you haven't been saying

I haven't wanted to hear
What you haven't wanted to say

Words left unspoken
Melt into nothing
Melting hope
Melting joy
Melting peace

It's really a sad and empty thing
When words don't belong anywhere
Because they've been left unsaid

When arms remain empty
Because they can hold no truth

When love is in turmoil
Because it doesn't have a place to rest

And time is in limbo
Always waiting, always waiting, always
waiting

Because ...

You're Magical Kiss

It began with a simple kiss
That became as unforgettable
As all the kisses ever since
It began and could not end

How could we have stopped those kisses
Those sweet tentative, searching kisses
Searching out each other's secret selves

How can we stop those kisses now
Those kisses that bind us
Pull us, beg us
For more.

There is nothing in my world
As splendid
As magical
As you're loving kiss.

Missing You

The eternal
Void
Can any one human being

Fill

It

Can you burn up the chill of the limbo that is time
Can you be the cure when you are not the cause

I wait impatiently to find out.

A Halo of Love

Yesterday we saw a red-gold halo
Circling the sun
As it went to sleep.

In the same way, after you are gone,
I stay warmed by a gentle halo left behind
From your glowing eyes,
Caring, flattering touches,
Sweet, forgiving kisses.

A halo that envelops me like a cocoon
Keeping our secret souls safe
Until we see each other again.

And so I go to sleep, a smiling sleep,
Protected by our halo of love.

Just Visiting

He was a stranger
In an exotic land
He thought he was staying
It was so warm, so loving, so exciting, so kind

There was laughter and lovemaking
Talking and lovemaking
Cuddling and lovemaking
Books and lovemaking
Singing and lovemaking
Dancing and lovemaking
Shared stories and lovemaking
Kissing and kissing and kissing
Always holding hands
Never letting go of the soft touch

But still he couldn't stay
He was a stranger after all
Even in his own skin
How could he adapt to a skin stranger still

He was just exploring
An adventure
Just a short visit

Wish he had told me
He was just visiting
Well, he did tell me
In a million ways

cont.

Thank you — politely

Don't do too much for me — I can't pay you back
I don't have much time — I'll be gone soon
Please don't bother — then I will owe you
Let me pay you for this — you are a stranger
That is so kind of you — I am a stranger
Don't raise your expectations — My love is not real
I didn't say what I didn't say — My words are not real
I don't know what I want — I am not real

I am a stranger
Just visiting.
You are a stranger
Never to be real
Just time enough
For a visit
A secret visit

Unable to travel beyond
The shores of the sanctioned
Unable
Unwilling
Whichever
Rooted in the land
Of the sanctioned
Un-reproachable
For such a holy decision
A comfortable land made real
Only by its rules
Diligently followed right to Death.

I Don't Like You My Love

I don't like you
   I don't like myself

You are buffeted
   By the winds of other people's whims

And I am thrown
   Into vortexes
   Stranger than my own

   I become a stranger to myself
Who I am
   What I feel
What I think
   Does not belong to me

   Foreign winds
   Foreign fears
   Alien struggles
   That I would
   Spit on easily
   Have the power to
   Render me powerless

I don't like your winds
I don't like that you
Don't blow them away
   From you
   From me

I don't like you, my Love.

Chronic Lovesickness

I think I'm being used
I think this dance will never end
I think I'm waiting for nothing

I feel like an idiot
I feel weak
I feel sad for myself, for him
I want it to be over — over!

A Turning Point

We have circled around ourselves
And around each other
Circles of fantasy
Circles of isolation
Circles of protection

Those circles have now been broken
And we're struggling to find a new way
Where heart and mind meet

We're not ready to give up
Nor are we ready to move ahead
Not until we find the way
That suits each of us

Hopefully that way will lead to
Each other again because that
Is what our hearts want
It's difficult to go where
The heart cannot go.

How do you leave your heart behind?

It's over ... once again

Once again I missed it
I didn't get it right
I misjudged
I mislooked
I mispoke
My heart misfired

I started that fire
And couldn't control it
And now its burning me up

It's my own fault
I stoked that fire, I prodded it, I fed it
Now it's killing me

I did it myself
I even saw when I lost control over it
But I didn't do anything
Fascinated by the strength of its force
Carried away by its beauty
Warmed by its heat
For my chilled soul

I didn't do anything
Now I suffer
A state I'm quite used to
More than I am with happiness.

No More Waiting

More days of waiting
And finally
The end
After the first end
After the many ends in between

Exhausted
Both of us exhausted
He, beaten by his past
So blinded by his past he could not see a future
Me, beaten by my past,
So hurt by my past I grabbed on to a shadow of a future

A shadow
    so unclear
    so yearning
    so in need
    so sad
    so sweet
    so loving

I thought I could give him strength
But I couldn't
Years of struggle for clarity and lasting love
A brave struggle
A hard fight
And now it's over

Exhausted I Am
Not even a shadow to keep me company

cont.

Parted   We   Are
We
Us

No   More

Holes in Souls

Verse One

I have a hole
In the bottom
Of my soul
But it's okay
I have control.

Verse Two

He bared his hole
In the bottom of his soul
I tried to fill it
But lost my control.

Verse Three

From time to time
He filled
The hole
In the bottom
Of my soul
But he got scared
Of losing his control.

Verse Four

He has a hole
In the middle of his brain
But it's okay
He's given up his control.

Verse Five

He's gone away
With his hole
At the bottom
Of his soul
And his hole
In the middle of his brain
And his wife
With all the control
Bye Bye.

Verse Six

Now I have control
Over my empty soul
Is that a good thing?

Him

What, where
Is the essence of Him?
I know
I will never know

I can explore
Territories
Here and there

I can taste
Bitter, sweet, milky trails
There, here
As they disappear

He sustains Himself
Taking from
Her, him, them

And when He laughs
With an up and down
Curve of his mouth
That says
There is no 'yes'
There is no 'no'
He's gone

Perhaps
I can find Him again
Here, there

Perhaps not
I won't ask
'Cause he won't tell.

The Right Trip

I'm not that bad
I'm not that stupid
I went on a trip with the right man
At the wrong time

Oh, but the trip was so right
I wish I had a return ticket
I wish I could hear once more
"Come back, will you?"

I Don't Know Why I Swallowed that Guy

I once was a girl
Who swallowed a Teddy

I don't know why
I swallowed that guy
I guess I'll die!

I once was a girl
Who swallowed an Eddie
Very heady
To have swallowed that Eddie
I swallowed that Eddie
To get over the Teddy

I don't know why
I swallowed that guy
I guess I'll die!!

I once was a young lady
Who swallowed a Mike
Yike!
I don't know why I swallowed that complicated guy

I swallowed that Mike
To get over that Eddie
I swallowed that Eddie
To get over the Teddy

I don't know why
I swallowed that guy
I guess I'll die!!!!

cont.

I once was a young lady
Who married a Paul
Indeed I did fall
And swallow that Paul
I swallowed that Paul
To get over that Mike
I swallowed that Mike
To get over that Eddy
I swallowed that Eddy
To get over the Teddy

I don't know why
I swallowed that guy
I guess I'll die!!!!

I once was a not-so-young lady
Who swallowed a Pierre
Ah, quelle romance avec ce gars!

I swallowed that Pierre
To get over that Paul
I swallowed that Paul
To get over that Mike
I swallowed that Mike
To get over the Eddy
I swallowed the Eddy
To get over the Teddy

I don't know why
I swallowed that guy
I guess I'll die !!!!

cont.

I am an older lady now
Who fell for a Luca
Oh why or why
Did I fall for one more guy
Before I die!!!!!

I swallowed that Luca
To get over my dear departed Pierre
I swallowed that Pierre
To get over that Paul
I swallowed that Paul
To get over that Mike
I swallowed that Mike
To get over that Eddie
I swallowed that Eddie
To get over the Teddy

I don't know why
I swallowed that guy
I guess I'll die !!!!!!

I didn't die !!!!!!!!!!!!
But I am very full !!!!!!!!!!!

Act 4

Maybe

Maybe

If I love you
Will you love me?
If you love me
Will I love you?

If I show you how
Perhaps you'll show me
If you show me how
Perhaps I'll show you

Maybe,
Maybe we'll love ourselves too.

Looking for Shooting Stars

You shouldn't look
For shooting stars

You have them don't you?

Yes, but you shouldn't look for them

He is afraid I will
Be disappointed

And then it burst across the sky
That shooting star —

It flew past
As if to say
Don't fear disappointments
Dare to hope and anticipate
I'm here.

Our Resilience

Our Resilience
    a life-giving force
    leading to growth and compassion

It comes from our relationships, experiences, reflections
    It comes from what we have chosen to strive for

Our resilience is inherited
    from our parents and ancestors

Our resilience is part of our collective humanity
    And we all have it in abundance!

Peace Doesn't Cost Anything

Peace doesn't cost anything
It just needs
Good humour
And a round table.

The Power of Stories

Analysis leads to Abstraction
which leads to minimilizing
which leads to trivializing
which leads to meaninglessness
which leads to extinction

Replace thought with experience.
experience is better shared
in the every day language of story

Receive the story as is
accompanied with the kind of love
that our grandmothers and grandfathers
would freely give us.

Finding Another Way

Conflict is a condition of human meaning

There is no antagonism
Unless
That is how we construct the world

There is no suffering
Unless
That is how we give meaning to something

Conflict can come from a flourishing
And can go to a flourishing
A different perspective
Can Illuminate
New Possibilities

The dance of fighting for justice
Is a dangerous dance
For everything we believe in
Can also hold the opposite

Within the space of
Multi-being
There is a wide range of opposition
Commonality is found
Because there is multiplicity

The way to "the truth"
Is to remove the search for certainty.

* Based on inspirational words by
Ken Gergen, Taos Institute

The Facilitator of Stories

In Africa
We eat out of one dish

Instead of mediating
Try "winnowing"*
Gather in a place of not knowing,
Enter a place with no agenda,
Abandon the idea
Of finding an agreement.

In Africa
We eat out of one dish.

In Memoriam: Samuel Mahaffy, Taos Institute

*Winnowing is a process that frees the grain
from the dirt by throwing it in the air.

Performing Coffee

Let us open doors
By performing coffee
In different cultures.

What will these doors
Open into?

So curious to find out.

Inspired by Stephen Holland-Wempe,
Taos Institute

My friend, Pamela

My friend Pamela
Starts slowly
Moves chaotically
From here
To faraway places

Sometimes she comes back
Sometimes she doesn't
And we lose sight of her

When she comes back
She is full of excitement
Sharing generously
The wonders of the worlds she has visited

She puts together this country
With that country
And creates a new country
One that is full of possibilities

Pamela's stories fill me with hope
Her simple manner of loving
With few demands, expectations or disapprovals
Just mutually exploring ideas and feelings.

If

If
You can
      Sit in the
Fire
      Sit in the
Nothing

      Sit in the
      Through

All will be well

If ...

Inherited Trauma–Cherished Burdens

The invisible child
With her invisible memories
Silently carrying the weight of history
Silently carrying the weight of her parents' suffering
Silently carrying the weight of the worlds' suffering

Without resentment
She carries the torch for her ancestors

Her sadness and resilience
Will create a better world
Will serve as a mantle
Protecting future generations

She smiles knowing she is strengthened
By her ancestors
Knowing she can say, "yes" to life.

(Based on my book: *The Inheritors,
Moving Forward from Generational Trauma*)

Cleanliness is Next to Godliness

The courtyard needs sweeping

But the courtyard's in the desert

Sweep on

Until Eternity then

Yes

Sir.

Facing the Future

Courageously vulnerable
That's me

Opening myself to risk
Nevertheless moving ahead

Anyway.

February

Shivering on the outside

A new glow of warmth glowing on the inside.

A Better Place

Today I am a grand, grand mama
Today the world is a better place
Today this little child
Gives meaning to the struggles of all the yesterdays

Today the world is quieter
Hushed by the awe
Of a sleeping child
Lulled by his father's song
Nourished by his mother's breast

Today the world took a breath
And gave space
In honour of his grand entrance
Into this grand world

How grand I am
How grand we all are
For the gift of life we
Give to one another

Today will make tomorrow
And the tomorrows thereafter
A better place.

I wish I were a "Yah-No" Mom

As time goes by, I wonder about the emptiness left behind by the "No"
I wonder about the sadness that grew and grew with each "No."

How can I say "No" to the children I love
When I can still feel the empty craters ground deep inside
With each denial still resounding in my head

Who will soothe them? Will they recover?
Will they be stronger, more resilient, and more resourceful?
Will they find their own way?

Do I have the courage to say
"Yes" to their ability to do it themselves,
"Yes" to my ability to sit with myself

I knew a woman who would answer questions with a "yah-no"
I never knew which answer she was giving, but things moved ahead
anyway.

I wish I had been a "yah-no" Mom
And my kids would never have empty craters to fill
They would say: "Mommy, I can do it by myself"
And, "Mom, you're not the boss of me,"
And, "Mother, I know what I'm doing."

cont.

I would simply reply, "yah-no,"
Because in the middle of yes-no
There are no fearful unknown futures
Theirs or mine

There is only
"I can choose"
       And if I get it wrong –
       "I can choose again."

De Gleckel/The Bell

As a child, you were called "de gleckel"
The bell,
And throughout your life
You have brought this bell of
Love and laughter with you.

Despite disappointments
Despite unhappiness
Despite difficulties
Through it all
The sound of the bell would ring.

Ring away the sadness
Ring away the tears.

We always loved to hear your laughing bell
Then we knew
That your strength would win out
No matter what came.

And then what?

When you destroy the bad side of yourself
Are you left with anything?

When you find the good side
What then?

Do you start all over again?
Creating new Good Bad
Destroying Bad Good
and on and on
Until death do you part
From your 1000 selves.

Visual Poem

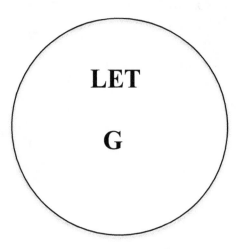

Meech Lake

Funny how a lake gurgles bubbles
Like a baby
Each lake takes its own shape
A shape the human eye cannot take in
All at once
The lake seems to contain
An understanding of its own
Unlike humans
It knows what it needs
Happy, comfortable in all the seasons
Always calm
Always beautiful
Able to reflect the world around it
Without losing its own identity
Able to be all ages and ageless

Funny how a lake gurgles bubbles.

Sitting on white Quartz

Sitting on white quartz
Looking inside
Asking myself: "What have I learned?"

I learned
    I can be alone
    Here
    Without feeling shut
    Out

    It doesn't mean
    I'm not being seen
    I'm merely
    In-between
    Myself
    and
    You.

Introduction to Life 101

Analyzing
Differentiating
Reflecting

    I think
    I feel
    I want

I think I'm procrastinating
I feel like a zombie
I want to get off this couch
That I've been on for five hours
TV zapper never far

    Circles of fear
    Holding me down

Yet
I know how to get out
It's easy
Be
Simple as that

    Let go the disappointments
    Let go the reflecting
    Let go the humiliations
    Let go the power trips
    Let go the helplessness

cont.

Let in the friendships
Let in the pride
Let in the authentic power
Let in the self-esteem
Let in a balanced self

Speak out my truth
With the natural flow
And rhythm
Of my voice
Embracing myself
Softly.

I Like Me and I Like You Too
— Reframing in Poetry

I like myself
Despite the winds of other people's whims
I keep my balance

I can find my own place
Wherever I go
Because I am with the person I belong to

I am no longer a stranger to myself
I know
Who I am
What I feel
What I think

I can listen to your struggles
Without needing to fill the void
For You
For Me

Those gales that blow our way
Will turn to cool drafts for our burned wings
If we look at them
With the cool, calm gaze of hope and possibilities

I like myself, and
I like you too.

The Immigrant

Great country this Canada
I go to the University at night
Nice place
Pretty girls
I better not get in the way

    Smiles

I'm very tired

    Looks around

Maybe I'll buy a nice modern suit

    Looks around again

This music these young people play
Not so bad
I'm happy here

    Taps foot

Wish I could get rid of this headache

    Rubs forehead

cont'd

I feel a little lost
Wish my family could see me now

Frowns

They wouldn't understand
But they would be proud

Must have cost a lot of money this building

Grimaces

Wish I had had this when I was young

Taps foot nervously

Hard this course I'm taking
My kids will be luckier

Rubs his brow

If another war doesn't come.

Haiku No 1

Ladies and Gentlemen
You have lost the wrestling match.
Because you fight dirty.

Haiku No. 2

Though you have many mysteries
I feel the whole of you
When you look at me.

Haiku No. 3

Nineteen Seventy-Five was that cold winter
That bore the fruit of my love.

Haiku No. 4   Laughter laughter all around
but not a smile to spare.

Haiku No. 5   Procrastination
from my destination.
Why?

Haiku No. 6   I would like to love you
if you would like me to
can you?

The Universal Song

Ours was a primal connection
Beyond head, beyond heart
A history shared at once
Beyond time.

Two bodies, two minds, two hearts
One soul
Piteously powerless without each other's force
Boundlessly powerful as One

Such love
As little understood as birth or death
More sought after than wealth

A waiting soul once it finds its twin
Breathes a different breath
Beats a renewed heart
And rests at last
Upon the pillow left behind by lovers
Throughout time
Upon which lovers hum
The universal song of sharing souls
Sharing the harmony of their essential Selves.

Questions without Answers

I once saw
I once thought I saw
I once remembered thinking I saw
I once remembered thinking I saw
I once remembered thinking I thought I saw
I don't remember what!

I once expected
I once hoped to expect
I remember hoping
I no longer hope to expect
I don't remember what!

I once saw
I once hoped
I once expected
I once wished
I don't remember why!

I was such a wise child
I am such a dumb adult....

But

When I grow down
Perhaps I will become
Rooted to the answers
To my questions
Which I no longer remember

And there it will be peaceful!

where's the exit, Jean Paul Sartre?

Solutions are not clear
And secrets make you sick
The whole is the sum of its parts
And the whole is in the part.

My shadow is within
My teddy bear is my area of illusion,
It keeps me safe from me
And it keeps me safe from not me.

One Size does not fit all
Does anything fit at all?

Two things I know
I exist, therefore I am, and
You exist, therefore we are.

The way we Do the world

Let us do the world
With a positive story
That will echo
Until it is heard
Around the world.

Travelling

Whoosh
Crouching in between the waves

 P
U

D
 O
  W
   N

Whoosh
Waiting, wondering
Feeling seasick
Whoosh

Swish
Perching on a leaf
On a tree twig
Rocking
To   and   fro
Swish

Swaying
In the tulip's womb
Breathing deep
The reviving honey
Swaying, sleep

cont.

Thrown into
An ant hill
Running
Back   and   Forth

Whoosh
Exhausted back in Masbelly
        Crouching in between the waves
        Waiting and Wondering.

HAPPY TRAVELLING!

About the Author

For over thirty years, Dr. Gita Arian Baack has been helping people to tap into new possibilities and to break out of limiting beliefs in her consulting and coaching practice. Her research on trans-generational trauma and on resilience led to her book, *The Inheritors: Moving Forward from Generational Trauma*, aimed at helping individuals and communities move forward from the aftermath of devastating events. Gita's keen observation of people, as evidenced in the *Poems of Angst and Awe*, continues to be one of her favourite activities.

Gita holds a Ph.D. from Tilburg University, The Netherlands, in association with Taos Institute, and an M.A. in Human Systems Intervention from Concordia University, Montreal, Canada. She lives and works in Ottawa, Canada.